THE METHOD
AND
THE MAGIC

EVERY LEADER'S GUIDE TO MAKING TRANSFORMATIONAL CHANGE HAPPEN

Laurie Axelrod and **Beth McDonald**

Enjoy!
Beth Al...
Laurie Axelrod

ISBN 0692437541

"The best-laid plans for change go awry when you don't successfully reach the folks involved. Axelrod and McDonald's insights about engaging and motivating employees, executives, and everyone involved in the change will help secure the full cooperation of your team. And their hilarious examples of how NOT to manage change are instructive as well!"

– Sharon Armstrong, Author of *The Essential HR Handbook* and *The Essential Performance Review Handbook*

"Change managers get to know employees' thoughts and feelings, but they often lack channels to effectively communicate their insights. At the same time, communicators have the tools to share the message, but lack the deep understanding that can make the message sing. Beth and Laurie combine the best change and communications strategies to create an indispensable guide for anyone leading organizational change."

– Patrick McCreesh, President of the Association for Change Management Professionals, Washington, DC

To our clients, who inspire us to do our best,
and to our team members, who simply are the best.

Laurie Axelrod and **Beth McDonald**

ACKNOWLEDGEMENTS

Like a successful change management or communications effort, the creation of this book was made possible by a dedicated team who saw the same Big Picture and worked tirelessly toward the goal.

We would like to express our sincere gratitude to all of the individuals who helped us conceive, write, and publish *The Method and the Magic*. Special thanks to our families for their support and patience, our parents for instilling in us a strong work ethic, Alyson Weinberg for helping us find our voice and inviting one of us to experience Lionel Richie with her, Betsy Rosenblatt Rosso for getting us over the finish line, Mimi Eanes McLaughlin for her creativity and flexibility, Kate Schmidgall and her team at Bittersweet Creative for creating our online presence, Lee Frothingham for continuing to refine our story for speaking gigs and for being our Brady Bunch fact checker, and Tamara Lucas for handling all the details and keeping us sane.

Finally, we thank our incredible team of consultants, for contributing their stories and experiences, challenging our thinking, and helping us raise the bar every day.

All of you make the magic happen.

Many thanks,
Beth and Laurie

There is an immutable conflict at work, in life and in business, a constant battle between peace and chaos. Neither can be mastered, but both can be influenced. How you go about that is the key to success.

Philip H. Knight, Co-founder of Nike

TABLE OF CONTENTS

FOREWORD

THE PEANUT BUTTER CUP MOMENT

During the 1980s, a commercial for Reese's® Peanut Butter Cups featured a pretty young woman walking down the street listening to music on her headphones while eating from a jar of peanut butter. (Who does that?) At the same time, a handsome young man is coming from the other direction, also wearing headphones, eating a chocolate bar. They bump into each other.

"You got your chocolate in my peanut butter!" she says. "Well, you got your peanut butter on my chocolate!" he replies. They taste the novel blend of ingredients and exclaim, "It's delicious!" and realize that peanut butter and chocolate are, in fact, two great tastes that taste great together.™

Our professional partnership was sparked in a similar way more than 15 years ago when we were each asked to help with different aspects of a major company turnaround effort. At the time this company, like many organizations, kept communications and change management separate. So, with Beth leading change management and Laurie leading communications, we launched our independent efforts to help the new CEO establish a series of organizational transformation efforts, something he called "The CEO's Top 10," a sort of Ten Commandments for the company.

As head of change management, Beth set out to understand what was needed to move the company from the current to the future state and to develop tools to help people embrace the changes. She gathered insights from staff interviews, surveys, and executive input, and pulled it all together. It was a somewhat unwieldy mass of incredibly important, incisive data. Meanwhile, as head of communications, Laurie began to conceive and distribute memorable, compelling messages that would drive the behavioral changes required to establish the CEO's new vision. She drafted memos and created lovely PowerPoint presentations. She honed the messages that leadership thought the audience should hear to lead the flock into the promised land of a better-run organization.

But unlike for Moses, whose leadership needed no more than a divine stamp of approval, getting the loyalty and buy-in this CEO needed to implement his Ten Commandments required deep insight into the hearts and minds of his people.

We worked diligently—and separately—toward the worthy goal of helping our CEO implement his fresh new vision. Until one day, Laurie happened to attend a meeting where Beth was reporting on her findings. She realized that from the treasure trove of information Beth had assembled she could craft a far more meaningful narrative. By using the insights Beth had gathered, Laurie could create messaging that gave their audience the precise information they needed to understand, participate in, and support the changes. Beth's message finally had a medium. And Laurie's media had a targeted, thoroughly vetted message. It was a clarifying "peanut butter cup moment." We had the work equivalent of two great tastes that taste great together. As for the CEO's new vision, we were able to create a cycle of targeted communication, feedback, and dialogue throughout the changing organization.

We realized that communicating about change based solely upon what executives *thought* their audiences wanted to hear (or what they wanted to say) hadn't gotten the whole job done. And trying to implement change in the absence of good communication—regardless of how solid the strategy and on-point the tools were—was like the proverbial tree that falls in the forest. If no one hears about it, does change even happen?

Making change happen is integral to the success of any organization and its ability to compete in today's marketplace. As Leon Megissen summarized Charles Darwin's theories, "It is not the strongest of the species that survive, nor the most intelligent, but the one most responsive to change." Change is critical to growth and success, yet there are few things leaders must do as challenging as managing change. The peanut butter cup moment led us to create a simple, integrated five-step approach to change management and communications which helps leaders face the daunting challenge of large-scale transition with confidence. With our method, which includes a bit of magic, leaders will begin to see change as the very instrument of their organization's ability to survive and thrive. As change management and communications professionals with many years of experience between us, we've successfully guided all types of organizations through complex types of organizational transformation—and we can guide you, too.

Our intention is to provide leaders with a simple but detailed plan to put their organizations on the path to successful organizational change—whether you're a CEO who needs to rally the troops, a project manager building a battle plan, or a staffer implementing change on the front lines. This isn't an academic tome. We're not going to spend a lot of time talking about leadership or learning theories. There are plenty of books that do that, and we've read and learned from many of them.

What we are going to present is something more practical—a realistic guide that outlines our strategy for successful change. We'll talk about why change is so difficult, and how and why it so often fails. We'll take you through our approach, using clearly explained tools and written in plain language that you can use to implement each step of our method and, ultimately, a successful transition. Along the way we'll share our experiences in the field and those of our colleagues and clients—victory in the world of change management, and also defeat. Some are success stories and some are cautionary tales; some are funny, and you can learn from those, too. We certainly did. We'll leverage the power of those stories to help you execute your transition successfully.

Our approach has been proven in organizations large and small, public and private. It can be adjusted to fit your culture. Because it speaks to basic human tendencies, it works in any organization. Our aim is to create a reference you can turn to at any point in the process—whether you're just starting out or you're in the thick of it and have run into difficulties. Through this book we hope to provide the answers, advice, and real-world ideas to keep you on the right track.

CHAPTER ONE

"YAY, YIKES!"

IT'S YOUR TURN

Every leader is at some point called upon to lead change. Imagine for a minute that it's your turn. You've been asked to spearhead an acquisition or reorganization within your company. Tapped to steer skeptical staffers through a major technological upgrade or to drive members to your organization's newly revamped online platform. It's a vast, complex project that could be a game changer for the company and for your career. Chances are you've been selected to lead this important initiative based upon your reputation, experience, expertise, or all three. That's good, right? So, how do you feel?

Excited? Nervous? You probably feel a combination of both. Something we call "Yay! Yikes!" Yay, because being chosen to manage change is a strong vote of confidence in you and your work. Yikes, because change can be daunting and often difficult—and many companies don't do it well. The stakes are high and the statistics can be discouraging.

In his book *A Sense of Urgency*, Harvard Business School leadership professor and change guru John Kotter estimates that nearly *70%* of change initiatives—a staggering percentage—fall short of their goals (Kotter, 2008). And that's if they're even completed. A study of senior executives across a variety of industries revealed 35% of organizations had abandoned a major business process change in the last three years and 37% reported their business change projects that did go through failed to deliver benefits (Logica Management Consulting, 2008). IBM conducted a survey of 1,500 change management executives on the success and failure rates of change projects which revealed a host of problems:

- Only 40% of projects met schedule, budget, and quality goals
- The best organizations are 10 times more successful at change than the worst
- Underestimation of complexity was listed as a factor in 35% of projects

The biggest barriers to success related to people: changing mindsets and attitudes, corporate culture, and lack of senior management support (IBM, 2000). Our own research backs this up. In 2013, we surveyed professionals across a wide range of disciplines about how their organizations handled change. While many acknowledged that the so-called "soft stuff," or people factors, were very important or essential, few felt their companies addressed these issues well. We'll share more of our findings in Chapter Two.

IT transition projects, in particular, can be unwieldy, expensive, and yield disappointing results. McKinsey and Company, in conjunction with Oxford University, conducted a study of 5,400 large-scale IT projects and found that 17% of them fail so miserably they threaten the existence of the company. In addition, researchers learned that large IT projects typically run 45% over budget while delivering 56% less value than predicted (Block, Blumberg, and Laartz, 2012).

Perhaps most dispiriting and daunting for leaders who must manage change is that when things go wrong, someone must be held accountable. Often it's the person at the top, the executive tasked with executing the change, who must be the fall guy or gal.

> **According to a recent study, unsuccessful organizational change is among the top reasons executives are fired. It accounts for nearly one-third of terminations, according to author and leadership expert Mark Murphy.** (Murphy, 2005)

Yikes! What's a potential catalyst like you to do? You could just dive in. You know your business; you have good support within your company. Who's to say you won't succeed? But, a word of caution, there are some very real reasons why change will be a struggle—and may even be a failure.

CH-CH-CH-CH-CHANGES
(TURN AND FACE THE STRAIN)

David Bowie intoned, "Turn and face the strain." In doing so he echoed abolitionist leader Frederick Douglass, who said: "If there is no struggle, there is no progress." Two diverse but wise sources describing the difficult nature of change. Change is challenging for reasons simple and complex, arising from human nature and the nature of the evolving American workplace. Here are three leading reasons why we think transitions can be difficult for even the savviest leaders:

- **Resistance in the Ranks:** Even when people logically agree change is necessary, they are hardwired to resist it. In fact, organizational experts Richard Beckhard and Reuben T. Harris devised a mathematical equation to show *the pain of the status quo must be greater than the pain of changing* in order for

$$C = [ABD] > X$$

WHERE **C** = CHANGE

A = LEVEL OF DISSATISFACTION WITH THE STATUS QUO

B = DESIRABILITY OF THE PROPOSED CHANGE OR END STATE

D = PRACTICALITY OF THE CHANGE

X = COST OF CHANGING

people to make a shift (Beckhard and Harris, 1987). It makes sense, and we all run this calculation every day. Still, when it comes to change, people rarely act according to plan or even according to their own best interests.

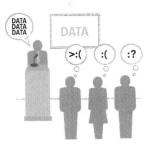

- **Sweating the "Soft Stuff:"** Change requires leaders to deal with people and their feelings, when it's a lot easier and neater to focus on data. Increasingly, confronting workers' anxieties and concerns plays a determining role in a leader's success. Employees today want to understand how change fits into the company's business strategy and, most importantly, why they should care.

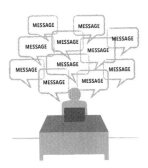

- **Too Many Messages:** Even when leaders address the thoughts and emotions of staff, communicating about them (or anything for that matter) has become fraught. People are buried in data, attention spans are shorter, and information is at everyone's fingertips. There are so many messages that only the most finely honed get through. Communicators who don't integrate change management practices into their approach can only speculate on how to reach and influence time-starved employees. More often than not, they get it wrong.

Problems with resistance, "soft stuff," and an overdose of messaging all can combine to make change highly uncomfortable for those involved. But if, as Katrina Kenison writes in *The Gift of An Ordinary Day*, "change is opportunity disguised as discomfort," you have to get comfortable with the discomfort (Kenison, 2009). And confront it. Help those involved in and affected by the change assess and address their reactions and, ultimately, embrace the opportunity. Aside from the challenges we just listed, which are inherent in any change, we believe the primary reason so many initiatives fail is that the folks responsible do not address those challenges with a strategy for integrating change management and communications.

Any internal initiative, large or small, can only succeed when these two key components work together like peanut butter and chocolate in our favorite candy. Change management—understanding what's needed to move an organization from the current to the future state and using those insights to help people embrace change—must work in concert with communications—conceiving and distributing memorable, compelling messages that will drive behavioral change. Many organizations keep these two disciplines separate, to disastrous effect. In the next chapter we'll explore how to address those challenges with a strategy for integrating change management and communications.

CHAPTER TWO

ONE-TRACK STRATEGIES DON'T WORK

Change management practiced in the absence of a solid communications strategy lacks the strength and power to truly succeed. Even the most clever messages are meaningless without real content to communicate. Unfortunately, many executives and organizations stick to a one-track strategy: practicing change management and communications separately.

A change management strategy without communications looks like this:

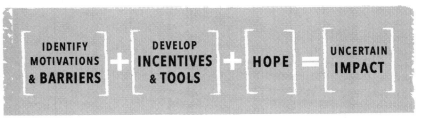

$$\left[\begin{array}{c} \text{IDENTIFY} \\ \text{MOTIVATIONS} \\ \text{\& BARRIERS} \end{array}\right] + \left[\begin{array}{c} \text{DEVELOP} \\ \text{INCENTIVES} \\ \text{\& TOOLS} \end{array}\right] + \left[\begin{array}{c} \text{HOPE} \end{array}\right] = \left[\begin{array}{c} \text{UNCERTAIN} \\ \text{IMPACT} \end{array}\right]$$

As you can see, the formula relies on the highly subjective and sadly ineffective tactic of hoping things work out. We're not knocking hope. It has its place, as do optimism and faith. Just not as part of your strategy. So what happens when change management happens in a vacuum? Excellent and insightful data is only helpful if packaged and communicated appropriately, which it rarely is. The four most common change management issues and missed opportunities that arise from separating change from communications include:

- **Stakeholder-Free Solutions:** People will support what they help create, so the saying goes. But do leaders take time to engage staff in the creative process? Mostly no. Doing so adds risk, takes patience, costs money, and can delay project timelines. Involving staff in making decisions also can make leaders feel vulnerable for reaching out.

- **Failing to Leverage Execs:** Executive support is critical to large-scale transformation, and most of us know how to secure initial backing. But knowing how to use executive support is another story. In fact, most project leaders are content to simply *have* an executive sponsor, but do not necessarily get that person deeply involved.

- **Letting Cultural Barriers Block Change:** Identifying barriers is a step in most major change processes. Removing them? Not so much. Often when someone labels a barrier "part of our culture," the issue gets dropped. Then the project team pretends that a genuine barrier, which could derail the entire project, doesn't exist or simply can't be overcome—instead of taking it on.

- **Irresistible Change?** Not quite: Removing resistance is never easy. Interestingly, the first place it appears is usually within the core project team. If the team is feeling unready—to communicate, to brief higher-ups, to launch—there is an underlying resistance that must be addressed. Keep getting bumped from your executive sponsor's calendar? Having trouble getting time with a colleague whose input is critical? That's not just coincidence. That's resistance.

We have a striking real-world example of a stakeholder-free solution. A large chain of home improvement stores appointed a new CEO. Upon taking the helm, he quickly saw the need for efficiency and cost-cutting adjustments. An avid numbers guy with a take-charge temperament, this leader set out to install self-checkout lanes and a sophisticated inventory control system in the stores. As he implemented these improvements, he also instructed managers to save money by cutting staff.

What this leader missed was that the chain's knowledgeable sales staff and personal-touch customer service were the exact characteristics that drove its strong revenues and repeat customers. If he had engaged his stakeholders, particularly his store managers, in the process of change, he would have gained valuable information and perhaps approached it differently. Instead, he alienated his staff and the changes flopped. Both results were contributing factors in his termination.

COMMUNICATIONS WITHOUT CHANGE MANAGEMENT

Working with a variety of clients over the years, we've seen that communications strategy that is uninformed by change management principles misses the mark. Here's the formula for that failed communications strategy:

$$\left[\begin{array}{c}\textbf{DEVELOP}\\\textbf{THE}\\\textbf{MESSAGE}\end{array}\right] + \left[\begin{array}{c}\textbf{PRODUCE}\\\textbf{MEMOS/}\\\textbf{ARTICLES}\end{array}\right] + \left[\begin{array}{c}\textbf{HOPE}\end{array}\right] = \left[\begin{array}{c}\textbf{UNCERTAIN}\\\textbf{RESULTS}\end{array}\right]$$

Uh-oh. There's that pesky hope again. Great if your favorite team's down a field goal but not so great as a communications strategy during organizational change. There are a number of ways in which this kind of one-track communications strategy can keep you from achieving a successful transition, resulting in problems ranging from dictator-style leadership to delivering a monologue instead of creating a dialogue.

Here's an example of one kind of communications snafu that we call **commander-in-change**, which made the resulting transition not at all "good to the last drop" as the coffee commercial says. Coffee figured prominently in this case of an IT and business consulting company that needed to make some big cost cuts. Not wanting to lay off staff (and risk signaling how dire the financial picture was), the folks at the top decided to instead cut lots of little stuff. Their hope was that all the small savings would add up to something big. They had a spreadsheet from the finance team to support their approach.

So the memo from the CEO came out: no more color copies, no more catered lunches, and, after analyzing the cost of offering free coffee in break rooms across the globe, there would be no more expensive Starbucks coffee. Discontent ensued. Employees gathered in the halls to discuss the memo. "How could they take away the Starbucks?" they cried. They began to wonder about the solvency of the company given that the leadership was taking such extreme measures.

The sound of human misery reached the CEO, who eventually relented and cut costs elsewhere. But morale had taken a hit. The coffee brand mattered. Having Starbucks (versus a cheaper generic coffee) made employees feel like they worked for a successful company that cared about its people. If executives had done their homework—and gathered the data prior to communicating—they would have known that. And, even if cutting the coffee expense were the right decision, having those insights would have enabled leaders to communicate the change in a way that helped employees understand. The CEO could have recognized the staff's sacrifice and asked them to pull together during austere times. Instead, the CEO alarmed and upset the staff.

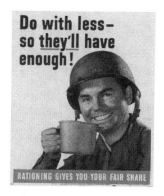

Credit: *Office of War Information poster, no. 37. 1943.*

DURING WWII, SACRIFICE IN A CUP

It shouldn't come as a surprise to any of us that a company changing coffee brands could cause such a stir. As a nation, we value our coffee. In fact, though most Americans in the 1940s were highly supportive of the war effort and willing to give up creature comforts for the good of the troops, doing without coffee was the part of rationing that tested their mettle most. When it was rationed in November 1942, citizens complied—but grumpily. Told to drink half as much of their favorite morning beverage so soldiers would have enough, some folks resorted to stretching it with chicory, boiling it on the stove, or using the same coffee grounds twice to increase their yield. Thankfully, President Roosevelt understood the importance of coffee to the nation and in July 1943 he announced the end of the coffee ration. Coffee was the first item to come off the rationed list, ahead of sugar, meat, and cheese (Loker, 2013).

THE BLUNDER OF POOR COMMUNICATION

Haven't we all received that cost-cutting memo from the leadership of our organization in the past (or been the one to send it)? Usually it goes badly. And why? When an initiative fails, it's common to blame poor communication. Research supports this too. Many surveys cite poor communication as the primary reason organizational transformations fail.

But what, exactly, does this mean? What separates good change communication from poor? Why do some messages inspire change and others fall flat or even alienate?

It's a dramatic disconnect, but sadly, one we see in practice every day. Here is a description of the important communications mistakes organizations make when authentic audience involvement and insights are missing.

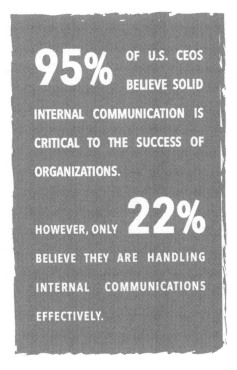

95% OF U.S. CEOS BELIEVE SOLID INTERNAL COMMUNICATION IS CRITICAL TO THE SUCCESS OF ORGANIZATIONS.

HOWEVER, ONLY **22%** BELIEVE THEY ARE HANDLING INTERNAL COMMUNICATIONS EFFECTIVELY.

- **Commander-in-Change:** Leaders giving orders without learning what it will take to get team members on board, expecting everyone to just fall in line.

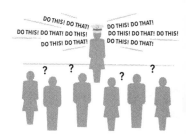

- **Wait, Wait, We're Almost There:** Waiting for the message to be perfect. Rather than involving folks early, or even signaling change is coming, leaders want to get every detail locked up first.

- **Huh? We're Gonna What?:** There's a message somewhere in all those memos, but no one can figure out what it is. This happens when the initiative didn't have a defined purpose. It was not adequately explained or tied to the company's vision.

- **Change Central:** Everything comes out of a single source—a good way to control message, but no way to engage people. When managers get the information at the same time as staff, it makes it harder for them to get behind the idea and sell it.

- **Monologue not Dialogue:** "Leaders who refuse to listen will eventually be surrounded by people who have nothing significant to say," said author and pastor Andy Stanley.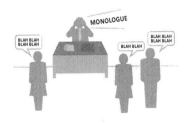
Leaders would rather deliver their great idea or brilliant message without testing it. Less risk.

Don't let these change management and communications traps scare you away from change. We'll have targeted advice for addressing all your project's potential pitfalls before they happen in Chapter Five, Remove the Guesswork.

HOW DOES YOUR COMPANY STACK UP?

Once we understood that organizational transformation requires clearly defined change management and communications plans woven together, we set out to gather data. What were companies doing well? Where were they falling short?

We reached out to upper-level professionals with more than 20 years experience in varying fields—including IT, government, the nonprofit sector, and hospitality—and surveyed them about their experiences with effective (and sometimes not so effective) change management and communications strategies.

The answers were telling. While the vast majority of respondents believed change management and communications strategies were essential to organizational transformation, many felt that their companies were not adequately putting these strategies into practice (see complete results in Figure A, pp. 26-27):

- **83%** of respondents said working with stakeholders to get consensus about vision, tagline, and success criteria was essential, but **more than half** conceded their companies did not do it well enough.

- **More than two-thirds** said using multiple communications channels to share changes was essential, but **more than 35%** said they did not do so.

- **About 70%** said that testing messages prior to rolling them out to a big audience was crucial, but **50%** said they did not put the strategy into practice successfully.

- While nearly **three-quarters** believed in being truthful with employees as early as legally permissible, **only 30%** said they did this adequately.

- A full **three-quarters** of respondents felt involving an executive sponsor was critical to success, but a mere **quarter** felt they did this sufficiently.

No matter how you might answer these questions for your own company, there's always room for improvement and no more crucial moment for it than when you launch a major initiative. Doing it right requires a lot of work, and unfortunately, there's no magic wand to wave. Well...maybe there is.

Fig. A *When leading transformational change initiatives, how important do you consider the following using the scale provided below?*

HOW IMPORTANT ARE THEY?

STRATEGY	Not important	Important	Very important	Essential
Working with key stakeholders to agree on vision, tagline, and success criteria	0%	3%	15%	83%
Conducting a stake-holder analysis	0%	13%	38%	50%
Holding stakeholder focus groups	3%	25%	28%	45%
Providing the full truth to employees as early on as legally possible	0%	13%	13%	74%
Testing your messaging on a small subset of stakeholders before sending it out to all impacted employees	3%	25%	30%	43%
Creating a plan for each of the stakeholder groups	0%	10%	33%	58%
Involving an executive sponsor	3%	3%	20%	75%
Using multiple communications avenues to share the changes	0%	13%	20%	68%

When implementing transformational change initiatives within your organization, how well are the following being done using the scale provided below?

HOW WELL ARE THEY BEING DONE?

STRATEGY	Not well enough	Well enough	Very well	Extremely well
Working with key stakeholders to agree on vision, tagline, and success criteria	51%	23%	21%	5%
Conducting a stakeholder analysis	33%	39%	23%	5%
Holding stakeholder focus groups	40%	29%	24%	8%
Providing the full truth to employees as early on as legally possible	35%	30%	19%	16%
Testing your messaging on a small subset of stakeholders before sending it out to all impacted employees	44%	36%	13%	8%
Creating a plan for each of the stakeholder groups	44%	26%	21%	10%
Involving an executive sponsor	21%	26%	23%	31%
Using multiple communications avenues to share the changes	36%	28%	21%	15%

CHAPTER THREE

THE METHOD AND THE MAGIC

WHY INTEGRATION WORKS BEST

How to succeed where others have not? That's the multi-million dollar question we've seen even the most seasoned, charismatic, and talented CEOs struggle with. Large-scale change requires flexing some different muscles. Muscles to do the heavy lifting of getting teams to envision the new organizational landscape and engage in the process of change. Muscles to execute intangible goals that may feel intimidating at first, such as overcoming doubt and cynicism. Muscles that take talented leaders—who are dynamic, potent, and successful in their daily work—to the next level, as successful change agents.

Some of what we're saying might not seem new. Many researchers have emphasized the importance of effective communication and change management in achieving large-scale change or transition. In fact, our approach is rooted in change management research and built upon foundations laid by thought leaders in the field. In our daily practice, we draw upon many of the familiar change models, for example, John Kotter's eight steps from *Leading Change*, William Bridges' theory in *Managing Transitions*, and Edgar Schein's work in *Organizational Culture and Leadership*.

The method and the magic approach works because it provides effective messaging that speaks to people's needs and provides the tools to overcome obstacles. Based on common-sense principles, informed by the best thinking in our field, it's much more than a method. There's an element of magic that comes from integrating change management and communications practices and it leads to knowing your audience, listening to their needs, and being creative in how you reach them. Unlike many magicians, we're willing to reveal how we pull the rabbit from the hat—and to teach today's leaders to manage organizational transitions with confidence and the tools to engage their audiences effectively.

In contrast to what we've already shown you, the method and the magic approach looks like this:

Notice there's no need to hope things will work out or close your eyes and throw messages like darts, praying to hit the bull's eye. The seamless combination of change management and communications ensures your messages will be well-vetted and on target. Over the course of the book we'll go in depth into each step to ensure you gain a full understanding of how to implement it. For starters, here's an overview of each of the five steps of our method—plus the magic that makes it happen.

Step One:
BUILD THE BIG PICTURE

In the first step, we show you how to shape the vision and determine what success will look like from the perspective of those involved. We show you how to gauge readiness and develop commitment from the project team.

MAGIC: Recognize that there is no ideal vision. Perfectionism is an impediment to change. Remember that the process of defining the vision, which includes who you involve in that process and how you engage them, is just as important as the end result.

Step Two:
REMOVE THE GUESSWORK

Now it's time to identify critical stakeholders and group them into four distinct categories: Advisors, Champions, Implementers, and Impacted Groups, and determine how the change will affect them.

MAGIC: Be collaborative. Share the big picture and gather reactions, input, and concerns from your stakeholders. Here's a big one—don't do a stakeholder analysis without members of the stakeholder group in the room.

Step Three:
GET THE MESSAGE RIGHT

Next, develop a balanced message that is visionary, believable, relevant, and instructive, using insights from the stakeholder analysis.

MAGIC: Take the time to share messages with a smaller group first. Even the most seasoned executives have been burned by neglecting this test phase. Find out how the message will sit with your intended audience before you press "send." What you learn could save a career—perhaps your own.

Step Four:
PREPARE THE STAKEHOLDERS

Then, create and deploy a plan that prepares each stakeholder group for the change. Your plan may involve developing training, tools, and quick reference guides.

MAGIC: Don't start with this step. While all projects include tactics to reach those affected by the change—issuing memos and FAQs, training, etc.—the magic is in doing the other steps before you create those things! Remember

to build the big picture, remove the guesswork, and get the message right first. Otherwise these materials are likely to fall flat.

Step Five:
EVALUATE THE RESULTS

To create your scorecard for success, integrate the expected business benefits of your initiative, the desired behaviors of each group, and the definition of "prepared" for each group. Together these measures—some qualitative and some quantitative—define success.

MAGIC: If you followed the first four steps, you were defining success each step of the way, continually taking the pulse of your transition. Nothing should come as a surprise to you and you should be enjoying the benefits of successful organizational change and communication.

CHAPTER FOUR

BUILD THE BIG PICTURE

IF YOU BUILD IT

In the 1989 film *Field of Dreams*, Ray Kinsella is walking his cornfields. He hears a voice saying, "If you build it, they will come." He imagines a baseball diamond with players fielding pop-ups, and fans coming from miles away. At first, everyone thinks he's nuts to build a baseball diamond in the middle of an Iowa field. (After all, he's talking with ghost ball players.) His vision does, indeed, seem far-fetched, but he works hard to share it with those he needs in his corner in order to realize it—including his wife and an idiosyncratic author, Terrence Mann, whom he meets on his journey.

Ray manages to convey why the vision matters—that celebrating the lives and talents of long-gone ball players is important. And slowly, but surely, the naysayers come to see (and hear) things his way. His wife spots a player in an old-fashioned uniform in their field. Terrence attends a ball game with Ray and hears the same otherworldly call to action Ray does.

Ray's wife, who initially saw his project as a financial risk—the loss of crop income—now sees it as a potential financial boon. It's she who proposes they charge money for people to watch the games, believing, correctly, that folks will pay to relive their childhood innocence. She agrees to plow up their crops and build the field. The ghostly players arrive, and enthusiastic spectators show up to watch them play. Ray has successfully shared what his mind's eye has seen and motivated others to help build his dream field, ushering in a fitting and poignant resolution to the plot.

Although it's a magical example, this is, in a sense, what you need to do to ensure the success of your transition. Time and again studies reveal, and change management literature teaches, that having vision and sharing it is a key—if not the key—component to a successful initiative and a successful leader.

THE IMPORTANCE OF SHARED VISION

According to one *Harvard Business Review* article, a visionary leader is something teams value greatly. When tens of thousands of workers around the world were surveyed about the qualities they most admire in a senior-level executive, 88% said that he or she should be forward-looking, or visionary. According to one well-respected executive cited in the article, when he requested feedback on his leadership from his team, one member responded eloquently, "You would benefit by helping us understand how you got to your vision. We want to walk with you while you create the goals and vision so we all get to the end vision together" (Kouzes and Posner, 2009).

According to organizational learning expert Peter Senge, author of *The Fifth Discipline: The Art and Practice of the Learning Organization*, leaders must translate their personal visions into shared visions in order to galvanize an organization. "The practice of shared vision involves the skills of unearthing shared 'pictures of the future' that foster genuine commitment rather than…compliance," he says. "In mastering this discipline, leaders learn the counter-productiveness of trying to dictate a vision, no matter how heartfelt" (Senge, 1990).

> We once told the CEO of a large organization that the first step to success is developing a shared vision with the staff. Common sense, right? We thought so, too. So you can imagine our surprise when he crafted his own vision, created a PowerPoint, presented it to staff in an uninterrupted monologue, and told us:
>
> "That's already done. I have a vision and I shared it with them."
>
> [EXAMPLE OF WHAT **NOT** TO DO]

A well-defined shared vision establishes why change is necessary and what the end goal looks like, including desired outcomes and benefits. While it may seem paradoxical, a good vision should be rooted in the organization's history and grow organically from the current state as much as possible. When the vision for the future is grounded this way, it becomes credible. Consider the value provided by this statement describing the vision for a technology and human resources transition by one of our clients: "When our employees grow and excel, so does the company. Through the new training portal, staff can set their professional development goals and access a recommended curriculum to guide their training decisions. The integrated technology platform implemented this fiscal year will provide a solid foundation for the new learning portal."

While the first sentence shows the value of the change, the second demonstrates how it is grounded in the company's established situation, decisions, and values. The portal is part of a longer-term technology vision and will be built on a successful foundation familiar to employees.

> "The best way to lead people into the future is to connect with them deeply in the present. The only visions that take hold are shared visions—and you will create them only when you listen very, very closely to others, appreciate their hopes and attend to their needs."
> Jim Kouzes and Barry Posner (*Harvard Business Review*, 2009)

THE VISIONING SESSION

When we help clients through organizational transitions—whether it's an IT overhaul, the introduction of a new system or process, or a complete reorganization—we conduct a visioning session with the project team. As we help leaders share their visions for change, we create an opportunity for debate, dissent, introspection, and discussion. Nagging concerns are surfaced as project teams deliberate on the reasons, benefits, risks, and success measures of the change.

Our visioning session has four components that we will go into in greater detail:

1. Agree on the vision.
2. Gain team commitment.
3. Create a project icon or tagline.
4. Define success.

The result of conducting a visioning session with your project team will be a clear, compelling, consistent, and, most importantly, co-created vision. A preview of the future state that vividly demonstrates what has yet to be created, like the vision Ray shared of his baseball field.

> When we surveyed professionals they said it was essential for change leaders to agree on a vision, but admitted that their organizations seldom do a good job of building that consensus.

We promise that if you invest the time and energy in building a clear, shared vision—and in involving others in shaping what could be, it will pay off exponentially. As Pat Williams, author of *How to be Like Walt: Capturing the Disney Magic Every Day of Your Life*, says:

Though Walt envisioned Disney World in Florida, he died before it was built. On opening day in 1971, almost five years after his death, someone commented to Mike Vance, creative director of Walt Disney Studios, "Isn't it too bad that Walt Disney didn't live to see this?" "He did see it," Vance replied. "That's why it's here."

(Williams, 2004)

AGREEING UPON THE VISION

In order to get "there," your team needs to understand and agree upon where "there" is. So, the first step in our visioning session is getting the team to consensus about the future state. We've created a number of questions to guide you. Spending time working through them as a group and building agreement around their answers accomplishes two things. One, it helps build the framework for the project's message platform (a concept we will discuss more in Chapter Nine, Get the Message

Right) and two, it builds engagement and clarity within the team. In other words, a visioning session helps shape your communications approach and it's a critical change management activity. That's the magic of an integrated strategy!

SAMPLE VISIONING WORKSHOP QUESTIONS

1. How is this work linked to the organization's strategic objectives and values?
2. What current or anticipated need are we addressing—or in other words, why the change?
3. What's changing?
4. What are the benefits?
5. What are the risks of not changing?
6. How will we know when we're successful?
7. How does this change tie in to other current or future initiatives?
8. Who is driving the change?

GAINING TEAM COMMITMENT

Once you have worked through step one (build the big picture), you should have a clear idea of where your team is headed. Now it's time to solidify their allegiance to the common goal. Significant change requires sustained commitment from motivated and sometimes daring team members. Yet, even when you do everything right, you may find the biggest barriers come from within your core team.

It's counterintuitive, but not at all uncommon, that the very people tasked with leading change resist it most. Why? High-performing teams, those trusted to lead transformational change, are composed of people who want to make a difference. They need meaningful work and they follow leaders who offer projects that matter. With transitions, especially complex and important ones, you must have people like this on your team.

But smart, motivated people question everything. They find holes and see deficiencies inherent in any program or technology solution. At some stage in the project doubts and anxiety will, therefore, necessarily creep in. The team will question their ability to support the new program. They will see the far-reaching impacts and wonder if they have the strength and authority to make change stick. Their commitment will wane. We see these issues all the time, and yet the project team is often the most overlooked in terms of resistance.

It's critically important to remember that the team that comes up with the vision may not automatically be committed to seeing it through.

In our experience, you've got to secure team buy-in by providing a safe environment for team members to share and troubleshoot their valid concerns. To start this process, we conduct a personal commitment assessment that explores reactions to several statements.

Many of our questions come from a diagnostic tool in Dan Cohen's *The Heart of Change Field Guide*. We ask questions from the personal commitment assessment such as:

- I feel strongly that this change is the right thing to do.
- I have the physical and mental stamina to see this change through to the end.
- I am willing to make compromises and handle setbacks that may occur along the way.
- Although I am busy, I have enough room on my plate to take an active role in leading change.

Next we ask team members to jot down the reasons behind their responses and share their reactions with the group. Our goal is not to call anyone out or put them on the spot but to create an environment where staff feels comfortable airing their feelings. It's important to make sure that team members who harbor doubts or face political pressures feel safe expressing their concerns openly with colleagues.

CREATING A PROJECT ICON OR TAGLINE

We've talked about the importance of co-creating a vision with your team and solidifying their resolve for the task at hand. Now how do you ensure mutual goals stay top of mind for those who must implement them?

Luckily, your brain already knows how to do this—and it's pretty cool. Have you ever bought a new car, and as soon as you drive it off the lot suddenly it seems that you see that same car everywhere? Buying a new car doesn't mean there are more cars on the road like yours. What really happens is that when you buy a new car your brain's Reticular Activating System (RAS) creates a new category for you to notice that same car model.

The RAS is pretty selective: with all the thousands of stimuli we confront every second it decides what to notice and what to ignore, like a filter between your conscious and subconscious mind. Here's an example of the RAS in action from Beth's personal life.

"I was on the phone waiting for customer service to pick up and needed to leave the room for a minute. So I put the handset on speaker next to my then two-year-old sitting in his high chair. Suddenly, I overheard the representative come on the line. **"May I help you?"** she said. Before I could get back to the phone, my son replied, "May I have chicken nuggets, a milk, and a toy, please?" Apparently he used his little RAS to recall his drive-through experiences and come up with the proper response to "May I help you?"

So what does that have to do with successful organizational change? **It's simple.**

Whether it's a phrase you hear with each visit to the drive-through, a symbol that compels you to recycle, or an image that encourages you to not only buy a certain kind of sneakers but lace them up and go for a run, taglines and graphics are powerful ways to reinforce ideas. You can program the RAS with anything that creates a memorable visual or auditory stimulus. If you do it right, every time your team sees a particular visual or phrase they remember what you are working toward.

The magic of our integrated approach is that as you're galvanizing and fortifying your team (change management) you also are communicating and reinforcing your goal (communications). Here are two ways to make it happen:

1. A graphical depiction of the vision or a true "big picture"
A single visual, jointly built with all team members, can serve as an icon for the program's promise. This visual touchstone will remind the team of achievements to date and where the initiative is headed.

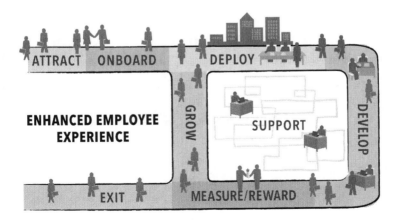

(See sidebar on page 47 for a description of how this came together beautifully for one client.)

2. A tagline or rallying cry

Another way to build the big picture is with words. Gather the troops to brainstorm words that summarize your vision. This might seem difficult. How do you boil a complex project down to a few memorable words? If your team finds itself challenged by this task remind them of these memorable words from Albert Einstein: "If you can't explain it simply, you don't understand it well enough."

We once worked with a business unit leader as he defined a new go-forward strategy for his organization. In addition to shifting the product direction and market focus, he also wanted to shift the internal culture. His goal was to continually encourage his team to be more thoughtful, focused, collaborative, and steadfast as they approached the change. In this case we used the tagline, "Think, Link, and Don't Blink!" which he posted on the door to his office and used in numerous conversations. The memorable tagline became part of the standard language of the organization and impacted the actions and decision-making of his entire team.

DEFINING SUCCESS

As the final step of your visioning session, you need to ask your project team one more question:

How will we know when we're successful?

It's a simple question, but the answer is complex. So let's spend some time on it. Here's an illustration. Imagine you're helping your 10-year-old with her math homework. She's struggling with adding unlike fractions and is getting frustrated. You get her to persevere, to stay at the kitchen table and complete the work. It's pulling teeth the whole way and, even with your assistance, she makes quite a few errors.

In the end, though, your daughter feels successful—and she should—because she finished the job. Great! But perhaps not everyone shares her view. Perhaps you do not because you define success differently. For you it may not be enough to get homework done; you want her to get it done independently. Maybe the teacher does not see it as a win, either; she has important standardized tests coming up and your child's C- on her homework indicates that the class may not be ready. Success looks different from different perspectives and nowhere is this more evident than with organizational change.

So, how will you really know when an initiative is successful, when the vision you worked so hard to hammer out has been realized? Well, you don't—unless you take the time and energy to define success at the beginning of the process. That's why we suggest you address it head on in step one of the method and the magic: build the big picture. Gather your team and find out what their endgame is. What will make this initiative a success for them?

Traditionally, communications professionals lack the overall perspective and ability to gauge whether their messages were effective beyond just being read. Those with a change management orientation may see behavioral change as their primary goal—simple awareness is not enough. In fact, it's not unusual for those in charge of communication and change management on the project team to define success in those functions independently from one another and independently from the project's business goals. And why not? If the memos and briefings occurred on time and awareness of change was high, then communications efforts were successful, right? Likewise, if people let go of the old and started behaving as needed to embrace the new, then the change management did its part, right?

Not so fast. These are red herrings—things that make it appear that success has been achieved when it has not. We've had many pointed debates with colleagues about whether they are valid signs of success. Let's take the example of a large-scale IT implementation, perhaps a new payroll system. Most folks would declare victory if employees continue to get paid. No one skipped a check or took a loss. But, do people like the new system? Is it user-friendly? Can they access the information they need about taxes or health care deductions easily? Not so much? Yes, the software is in and working according to requirements. But it's not producing business benefit because readiness and user acceptance doesn't reach full potential.

Our philosophy on measurement is that you simply cannot separate change management and communications measures from the overall business impact of the change. That's the magic of an integrated approach—and the challenge. If the change didn't realize its goals and deliver results, then the communications and change management leaders must accept some responsibility. Success in these areas cannot be declared no matter how many memos, focus groups, training classes, or town halls occurred. Success cannot even be declared if a new system works but doesn't deliver its full potential because of user adoption issues. Once you've established how success looks from your project team's perspective you can move to the next step of the method and the magic: remove the guesswork. We'll return to this tricky question of gauging success when we analyze our stakeholders. Part of defining the success of the business result is defining what it will look like for each of these groups—and working to reach those benchmarks.

No one said change is easy. In fact, in our experience, if it seems easy you're probably missing something really important.

THE ART OF VISION BUILDING

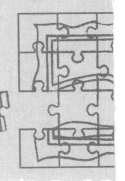

One of our favorite illustrations of building the big picture occurred when we worked with a client to create a shared vision for their organization. We suggested they build the big picture, quite literally. We partnered with a team from Catalyst, a creative business consulting firm, to listen to the executives describe what their vision looked like, and then help us create it.

The designer then fashioned a huge billboard-sized poster, 36 feet by 18 feet, a visual representation of their future state. The poster was then broken into small, unrecognizable pieces that were transposed onto individual one-square foot canvases that fit together like a puzzle. Each was a paint-by-numbers outline of a portion of the larger image.

The top 300 leaders in the organization were asked to work together in teams to paint the canvases. Without ever having seen the final artwork, each team was given a square section, paint, aprons, and an hour to paint their section of the artwork. They were told which teams were working on the adjacent canvases in the puzzle and were asked to work with them to mix and share paint colors and ensure the pieces fit together.

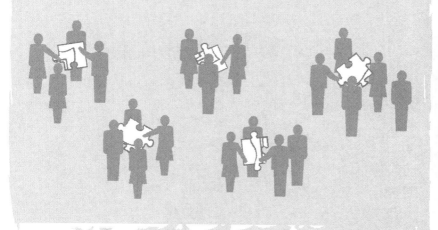

At first, teams were not so enthusiastic. They mocked the exercise and complained they were getting behind on their real work. But slowly each team started to collaborate. They became excited when they found a connection. Colors started to blend and shapes started to take form. When time was up, we collected the work to let it dry. Later that day, we called everyone together again and unveiled the completed billboard.

When the curtain dropped on their huge wall art, there were gasps around the room. The team understood how each of their efforts contributed to a larger goal and saw that the end result reflected all of their talents and hard work. Even more exciting, they now understood how they could apply the same hybrid of dedication to task and collaboration to their upcoming transition. They had a vision of what the future looked like. One they had helped create. They had literally built the big picture.

CHAPTER FIVE

REMOVE THE GUESSWORK

DON'T FORGET ABOUT THE FLOWERS

In the movie *Ice Castles*—yes, it's cheesy, but it makes our point—Lexi, a young figure skater, is blinded in an accident and gives up competing. With the help of her boyfriend, Nick, she decides to make a comeback and fool the audience into thinking she is sighted. Lexi practices day after day to anticipate every potential obstacle and ensure she skates a flawless program. On competition day, she executes her routine perfectly, to rousing applause and a standing ovation, but trips and falls over roses thrown onto the ice by fans, revealing her ruse. Laments Nick, "We forgot about the flowers!"

Now picture your team. You've been toiling away diligently on a project for several months. You have anticipated technical issues and met project goals and milestones. Your solution is tested and ready for launch. But, as you prepare to go live, imagine one of the following scenarios:

- You learn halfway through a project launch briefing that this is the first time a key executive has heard of the change.

- You are ready to implement a new employee benefit, and realize neither the HR staff nor the help desk has been trained to handle staff questions.

- You convince the CFO to invite staff to attend training on the new financial system. The message creates confusion: staff members claim to have never heard about the change or its timing or objectives. The CFO's office gets bombarded with questions, and you're in the hot seat.

- You send out a note about what you think is a benign aspect of the change, and you quickly realize it touches a nerve with staff and threatens to sink the larger program.

You've forgotten about the flowers. When these situations occur, as they often do, months of clean skating across the project are overshadowed by one stumble—leaving your team bewildered and demoralized. Whether you've experienced a setback like this, or simply want to avoid one, you must anticipate these moments by identifying and understanding the needs of your various stakeholders.

For this reason, when working with clients we devote significant time to change-focused stakeholder analysis, something we call remove the guesswork, the second of our five steps, and in some ways the most important. We bring together the team for systematic and thorough brainstorming to ensure there is no stone—or bouquet of roses—left unturned.

While conducting a comprehensive stakeholder analysis is the critical exercise in removing the guesswork, you need to do some preparation before you get there. Understanding the different stages your people go through is an integral intermediate step.

THE EMOTIONAL AND PRACTICAL STAGES OF READINESS

"Plus ça change, plus c'est la même chose" is a well-known French proverb, meaning, "the more things change, the more they stay the same." A bit pessimistic, but accurate. Who hasn't heard people within their organization say that everything has changed but nothing is really different?

We hear this all the time and the message is clear: just because you have planted the seed of change—the office has relocated, the new performance management process has been launched, the updated organizational structure is in place—doesn't guarantee change has taken root. According to William Bridges, author of *Managing Transitions*, when this happens, people's feelings are the cause. He says that in order for change to truly occur, *transitions* need to happen. Change is situational while transition is psychological. "When change happens without people going through the transition, it is just a rearrangement of the chairs" (Bridges, 1991).

While we won't replicate Bridges' book here (it is a worthwhile read for any change management professional), we will highlight key concepts. Bridges believes helping people emotionally process the transition is critical if the change is going to function as intended. He also asserts that managing transitions is about helping people through three phases: endings, the neutral zone, and the new beginning.

How do you move people through the transition so they are open and ready to change—when you need them to be? Many years ago, Laurie was part of a team that helped a multinational company through a major organizational transformation. The company was looking to spin off a large division, one with innovative products and a well-known global brand, into a separate public company. Wall Street was thrilled by the idea, because the division had grown to the point that it was undervalued as part of the more staid parent company. The move made sound business sense. But company leadership astutely anticipated an employee morale problem.

Without the innovative division, the parent organization lacked a clear market identity. Employees who remained with the parent company might perceive that they were left behind—no longer part of an exciting and fast-growing company. Leadership was concerned about attrition and lack of engagement. Within the parent organization, the question senior leaders asked was, "How can we leverage the spin-off event to generate a sense of excitement among employees of the parent company and define the next chapter in the story of the 50-year-old parent corporation?"

It was a classic scenario in which employees needed to mourn a loss, move through the neutral zone, and embrace a new beginning. Working with the company historian, we helped write a book capturing the many impressive chapters in the company's history. We launched a global, manager-led program to encourage employees to submit their reflections, honoring employees' feelings about the coming change and setting the transition up for success. The hardcover book was intended to be a source of pride for employees, helping reconnect them to the past and remember which achievements marked their five decades of success. There was space in the book for employees to add their own stories and hopes. Paying attention to their emotions about the change paid off.

Honoring the feelings of those involved in the change is important. So, too, is awareness of the process of change each person must go through on a practical level. "Change is a threat when done to me, but an opportunity when done by me," says Harvard Business School professor and renowned leadership and change expert Rosabeth Moss Kanter (Moss Kanter, 1983).

It's true: time and again we've seen that when change is thrust upon people, without thought to the way humans process change, it just doesn't work. There are numerous models in change literature that illustrate readiness stages and how to lead your team through them to prepare for change. Interestingly, though, when you compare the models side by side, the differences between models are mainly in terminology and the number of steps.

Why? Because human beings go through the stages of change in predictable ways. No matter how many change management gurus study and label this process, the findings are the same. Rather than create yet another model, we frame the process in terms of the activities we must take stakeholders through in order to be ready for change. Stakeholders must provide input, understand the changes, and be prepared for how to behave differently.

> **"Resistance is always greatest when change is inflicted on people without their involvement, making the change effort feel oppressive or constraining. If it is possible to tie change to things people already want, and give them a chance to act on their own goals and aspirations, then it is met with more enthusiasm and commitment."**
>
> Rosabeth Moss Kanter, 2010

PREPARING PEOPLE FOR CHANGE

ACTIVITY	HOW CHANGE LEADERS SHOULD SUPPORT	STAKEHOLDER ACTION
Provide Input	Give them or their representatives an opportunity to be part of thinking through and developing solutions	Attend focus groups and offer reactions to change and means to achieve it.
Understand the Changes	Shape their understanding of what is changing, why, and the costs of not doing so.	Participate and thoroughly engage in meetings and with materials. Contribute honest feedback.
Be Prepared	Provide tools, information, and training to help them adopt the change.	Use the tools, information, and training to ensure a smooth transition.

Many of the well-known stages of change models can be useful. What's important from our perspective, as you move forward to identify your stakeholders and conduct your stakeholder analysis, is understanding the actions you need to take to move them through the change and set yourself up for success.

CHAPTER SIX

THE FOUR TYPES OF STAKEHOLDERS

Think about an upcoming change in your organization for a moment. You may think you know who your stakeholders are. You may even think you can categorize them easily. In fact, once you get going, you could have a long list. But what we often notice with clients going through a change is that they separate their stakeholders into groups *by function*. So, if it's a cost-cutting transition, they might say their stakeholders are the executives making the decisions, the financial team who has to trim the fat, the human resources folks who will have to let employees go, and it goes on from there.

We have learned, however, that categorizing stakeholders by function doesn't get you very far. It doesn't tell you anything about how the groups will be affected by the change or how you should prepare them. Whether you identify four or forty separate individuals or groups, we find they boil down to four categories that work across the functions of your organization:

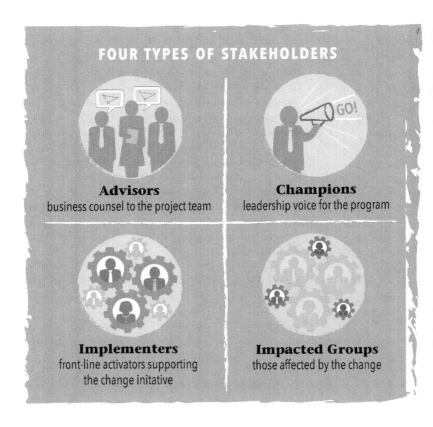

FOUR TYPES OF STAKEHOLDERS

Advisors
business counsel to the project team

Champions
leadership voice for the program

Implementers
front-line activators supporting
the change initative

Impacted Groups
those affected by the change

The magic in understanding the four categories is using these groupings to simplify your stakeholder analysis. The messages, desired changes, measurement, and tactics to reach the people within a category are similar. You don't need a million different plans for each type of employee in your organization—from the executive suite to the mailroom—just one plan for each category.

Meet the four stakeholder groups. We'll explore them in greater depth in Chapter Seven when we discuss how to prepare your stakeholders.

1. ADVISORS

Who are they?

Advisors are leaders who shape the program. They understand the business imperative for change; have a personal passion for the program, product, or service being launched; and are committed to its success. Advisors connect the dots of the change program to other strategic initiatives.

What is their role?

Advisors provide subject matter expertise for the change solution. They assist the project team in addressing potential resistance from stakeholders and advise the project team on removing cultural barriers.

2. CHAMPIONS

Who are they?

Champions are the leaders of the groups who are impacted by the change. They are credible authority figures who provide essential sustained support in the field, helping employees understand and adopt the change.

What is their role?

Champions are spokespeople for the change. They champion the solution, answer questions, defend unfounded negative criticism, and provide the on-the-ground communications support for the program to be successful.

3. IMPLEMENTERS

Who are they?

Implementers are members of your project team. They are responsible for putting your initiative into action. Implementers also include any group that will be responsible for supporting the execution of the change. Who they are depends on the type of change. For example, for a change to an employee benefit program, implementers might include human resources staff and help desk personnel.

What is their role?

It depends on the group. In our employee benefit example, help desk staff will need to troubleshoot issues and questions that arise, while human resources staff might need to advise on new benefit options.

4. IMPACTED GROUPS

Who are they?

Impacted groups are probably easiest to identify. They are the people who will need to do something differently because of the change. This group varies depending on the type of change.

What is their role?

Typically, impacted groups have a role in the administration of a new process. They may be required to use a new technology or product, perform their jobs differently, or provide customers with a new service.

Now that we know who your stakeholders are, let's talk about how to work with them to make your change a success.

CHAPTER SEVEN

UNDERSTANDING YOUR STAKEHOLDERS

Figuring out who your stakeholders are and exploring what they're about are key components of step two of the method and the magic: remove the guesswork. Stakeholders are broadly defined as a person or group with an investment, share, or interest in something. That covers a whole lot of people when you're dealing with organizational change. To determine who your stakeholders are, ask the following questions.

• Who must be engaged in the change?

• When must they be engaged?

• How engaged should they be?

Be sure to involve the core project team and your advisors in this step to glean a variety of perspectives and avoid leaving anyone critical out of the process. For complex transformation efforts, such as the acquisition of a new company or implementation of a new company-wide system, we suggest a workshop to identify stakeholders. For more straightforward changes, such as adding a new data field to a form, working with your project team and validating with executive sponsors will do the trick. Once you have the list of folks who need to be engaged, assign them to one of the four groups: advisors, champions, implementers, and impacted groups. You now have a complete stakeholder list and you can now conduct your stakeholder analysis.

THE STAKEHOLDER ANALYSIS

The goal of the stakeholder analysis is to identify each group's unique needs in regard to the change, with the end goal of taking them through the readiness stages mentioned earlier. The first step is to ask the project team what they believe to be true about each group. What we do next is an important but uncommon approach.

The magic is in bringing representatives from each stakeholder group together to validate or repudiate the insights of the project team and to answer additional detailed questions.

Notice in each of these meetings we ask ourselves what success looks like—just as we did in the first step: build the big picture. We are constantly asking ourselves this question and refining our answers. We are checking ourselves against these success markers along the way to stay on track.

For the first stakeholder session with the project team, we work to establish the basics about the impact of the change on each group. We do this by answering the following key questions about each stakeholder:

• What is actually changing for this group? Do they need to do something differently, such as access a system in a different way or follow a new process?

• Do employees benefit directly, such as having tools that are easier to use? Will the company save money?

• What is the pain of not changing? Will this organization be penalized if it doesn't change (e.g., if they don't upgrade to a new system will there be higher maintenance fees?) or will employees *not* benefit from a new program?

• How and when do we involve them in the program? When do we want input to shape our solution or a rollout plan?

• What are the best ways to reach you with information about the upcoming changes?

- Is there a negative impact on this group? For example, will the group receive less customization of the system for the greater good of the organization?

- What does "prepared" mean to this group? Do they need to be trained?

- What behaviors do we want from them? Do they need to speak differently, sell more aggressively, respond to customers more swiftly?

- What are the cultural challenges regarding these behavior changes? How do we shift the culture? Do they need to work in teams more, and if so, should we reward team performance instead of individual performance?

- How will we know when we are successful? What do they say means success?

In the next step, we conduct a session that adds actual stakeholder representatives to the meeting and we ask the following questions:

- What are your current perceptions? What are you hearing about the change?

- What would motivate you to support this change?

- How do you want to be involved in the change?

- Are there any short-term wins for this group?

- What are the barriers to this change and how would you remove them?

- What kind of resistance might we encounter from this group? How can we reduce the resistance?

- What do you need from us?

- What is your definition of success?

We write about these groups of stakeholders as if you simply identify them, ask them some questions, and build your plan. It's not that easy. Every time you bring people into the mix, your program gets more challenging. But it also gets better. In the next chapter we'll look at how stakeholders fall into distinct groups defined by how much they agree with and trust in the change—and offer ways to best deal with each of them.

CHAPTER EIGHT

SUPPORT, RESISTANCE, AND EVERYTHING IN BETWEEN

ARE THEY WITH YOU OR AGAINST YOU? (WE HOPE SO)

When Laurie moved her son into the dorm for his first year of college, she saw a frat boy handing out fliers and wearing a t-shirt advertising his fraternity that read: **Loved. Hated. But Never Ignored.** The wisdom of the shirt made her laugh and surprised her by its relevance to client work. You can't guarantee people will love a change or think it's the best of all solutions. You also can't guarantee they won't hate it and resist it the whole way. But, if they feel something, then they're engaged, and you need your people engaged in the change, no matter how they feel about it. When you know how they feel you can deal with it, which is always better than being ignored. Even people who start out with a negative opinion of the change are at least part of the conversation, which is a starting point for engendering their support.

ALLIES, ADVERSARIES, AND OPPONENTS, OH MY

Within each stakeholder group you are going to run into folks who are game for your program, totally against it, and somewhere in between. Of course, you'd expect to see variances in the reactions of your impacted groups. But, in addition, some of your advisors will be naysayers, some champions may be lukewarm, and often your implementers—the very people you need to be 100% on board—will be your most challenging program foes.

In his time-tested book *The Empowered Manager*, business consultant Peter Block talks about how stakeholders fall along a matrix of agreement and trust. He offers some terrific advice for managing them, wherever they fall on the matrix (see Figure B below [Block, 1987]). We think Block's paradigm is useful and recommend using it to categorize your stakeholders according to their level of agreement and trust. This approach is an excellent way to surface and deal with resistance.

Fig. B

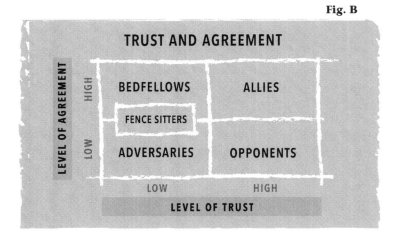

YOU'VE GOT A FRIEND IN ME

At the high end of the matrix, according to Block, you have **allies**. Allies have a high level of trust in your program team and high agreement with your plan. Allies can come from all stakeholder groups and can be valuable ambassadors for the program.

Tips for leveraging allies include:

• Let them know you value their opinions.
• Give them a forum to share anxiety.
• Ask for their guidance and support.

AGREEING TO DISAGREE

Next come the **opponents**. Block says these folks have a high level of trust in you but a low level of agreement with the plan. Because opponents trust you, they are easy to get along with. Allow them to challenge what you're doing so you can tweak the program, if necessary, to solidify and even improve your position.

Tips for engaging opponents include:

• Let them know you value their honesty and feedback.
• Tell them your plan in a neutral way to learn where and why they disagree.
• Ask them to help you identify some alternatives to address their issues.

THE SKITTISH AND THE SKEPTICAL

What about people who agree with the plan but don't trust you? These Block calls **bedfellows**. Because they agree with the program, the goal is to build trust. You want them to know you have no hidden agendas. It's important to commit to full transparency when dealing with bedfellows.

Tips for building trust with bedfellows:

- Acknowledge that there is some distrust in the relationship and that you want to work toward common ground.
- Be clear about their roles (e.g., keep us informed, take some sort of action, etc.) and, in turn, be clear about what you will do for them.
- Agree upon how to work together to implement this change.

NEITHER HERE NOR THERE

Someone who does not take a stand for or against us is a **fence sitter**. The easiest way to tell a fence sitter from the others is by their easy nature, comfort with conflict management, and patience. They will not take a stand and you might never be quite sure what they believe. You might waste inordinate amounts of time managing the fence sitter and essentially they won't go to one side or another because of doubt. They doubt the value of your project and so it is easier for them to take a wait and see approach.

Fence sitters are not worth a lot of our time and energy as there is little we can do to influence them. However, if you choose to deal with fence sitters, you want to:

• Let them know about the project vision, goals, and purpose.
• Ask them to express their opinion without judging them for it.
• Encourage them to take more time and ask them to identify what it would take for them to give their support.

THEY'RE JUST NOT THAT INTO YOU (OR YOUR PROGRAM)

Lastly, we have our **adversaries**. Adversaries have the potential to drain your energy and divert your attention. Don't let them. People become adversaries when attempts to convince them (as if they were bedfellows or opponents) have failed. Make sure you know they are adversaries before you begin working with them as if they are. But once you do, realize that the more you try to convince your adversaries the stronger adversaries they become. To neutralize them, you have to let go and stop aiming to persuade them. One option is to eliminate contact with them—make no demand, let them off the hook—and in certain cases this is the best route, but first you should:

• Let them know about project vision, goals, and purpose.
• Accept the fact that there is an alternative or even an opposing view on your position and communicate that.

Communicating is demonstrating understanding, not necessarily agreeing with the opposition.

- Take responsibility for any valid parts of their argument or your contribution to the problem they are concerned with. This will show your willingness to live out the values of your program, win the support of your adversary, and make it easier for bystanders to take your side.

WE HAVE SEEN SOME OF THE BIGGEST, LOUDEST, MOST VOCAL BEDFELLOWS AND OPPONENTS BECOME ALLIES–with some really hard work.

So where should you spend your time and energy? We have found that time with allies is well spent in order to enlist their support and learn what things you are not hearing. But you should not have to spend an inordinate amount of time with them. We suggest you focus your energy on your bedfellows and your opponents because you only have to work on building agreement or trust.

How to Work a Conversion

Both opponents and bedfellows have the potential to become allies, because as we've described, Block's model reveals that each has a strength you can build upon. With opponents, it's their general trust in the leadership. With bedfellows, it's their agreement with the program. Here's how we helped clients move opponents and bedfellows into the allies quadrant.

TRUST TURNS AN OPPONENT INTO AN ALLY

When we helped a large government agency launch a new organizational structure, our client knew there would be opponents and that they would come from inside her leadership team. One gentleman in particular had trust in the leadership but was vocal about his disagreement with the new plan. We suggested our client include him in designing a three-day offsite meeting that would launch the new organization. While it may seem counterintuitive, she parlayed his general goodwill and trust into hard work—and the result was a much better initiative.

Our opponent felt his input was valued and he got involved. He helped hammer out messages and choose content that would drive the messages home and prepare people for the change. His work behind the scenes allowed him to shape the areas of disagreement into something more palatable for his colleagues. In the end, he was one of the most powerful spokespeople for the change and agreed to be the emcee for its kick-off event.

AGREEMENT MAKES AN ALLY OUT OF A BEDFELLOW

In another agency, the project goal was to roll out a new system, replacing one that had been in place for three decades. Talk about a change management challenge! There were two main organizations involved in the change and both were stubborn, historically did not work well together, and were at each other's throats whenever anything new was implemented.

Our client was the leader of one of these organizations. While both leaders agreed the new system was the way to go, they didn't trust each other. Through a series of well-orchestrated meetings to discuss current plans, upcoming milestones, interdependencies, and risks to both organizations, we were able to help the bedfellow organizations move closer to becoming allies than ever thought possible.

At each meeting the program managers would present the current state of the initiative. At first these meetings ended in frustration and even finger-pointing, but as the meetings progressed and the bedfellows witnessed each other's goodwill and transparency, tensions lessened and issues were raised in a spirit of collaboration instead of accusation.

CHAPTER NINE

GET THE MESSAGE RIGHT

"HELLO?" DO YOU WANT TO BE "DANCING ON THE CEILING" "ALL NIGHT LONG?"

You may be wondering how Lionel Richie lyrics made their way into *The Method and The Magic*. We apologize for another 80s pop culture reference—this time to Lionel's music—but we recently learned he's a genius at our third step: **get the message right.**

We know this because one of us (we won't say which) recently attended one of his concerts. She says, though we're not sure we believe it, that she was attending it "ironically." It seems her plan was to stand apart and observe, maybe draw conclusions, as business consultants are wont to do. She wasn't planning on singing "Brick House" at the top of her lungs or vividly remembering the eighth grade formal where she slow danced to "Endless Love." But Lionel's messaging—and the magic of getting it right—shall we say, influenced her behavior.

It was clear he had done great prep work. He had analyzed his stakeholders and knew what they wanted and needed from the performance. He had definitely done his research. He took the stage and immediately acknowledged his stakeholder groups. "I know who's here tonight," he said. "I've got the Commodores fans—you know who you are. You're going to want to hear 'Three Times a Lady.'" The audience went wild.

"And then there are the fans of my solo career in the 80s." A segment of the crowd roared. "How about some 'All Night Long?'"

"And then there's the other group. The kids who came here because their parents played my music when they were growing up. And you love it all!" There were hoots and hollers all around.

He then laid out a message he knew would resonate: he said that no matter which category of fan audience members fell into he wanted them to *remember where they were, what they were doing, and who they were with* when they heard their favorite songs.

He spoke from the heart, telling the true stories behind some of his best-loved melodies. He promised to sing everyone's beloved songs and checked in with the crowd, "Does that sound good to you?" Lionel played enough songs to satisfy each group, all the greatest hits and more. Pretty soon the whole audience was singing the same tune.

What Lionel did in his concert echoes our own views about how to get the message right:

- Build powerful, balanced messaging.
- Make it mean something.
- Tell the truth.
- Test your messaging.
- Get everyone to say (or sing) the same thing.

All of which we will teach you to do.

And when he was done, a certain nameless business consultant realized that she had remembered where she was, whom she was with, and what she was doing within the first few notes of each song.

BUILD POWERFUL, BALANCED MESSAGING

Developing messages that reach the heart and mind of your audience and compel them to do things differently is an art form. To paint your messages vividly and brightly you need a well-prepped canvas. Compelling messaging requires deep insights into your stakeholder group, insights that are gained through the prep work you did to remove the guesswork (as discussed in the previous chapter). This is how integrating change management practices with communications begins to pay off.

Any message that is powerful enough to drive behavioral change requires four key elements in balance. It must be visionary, believable, relevant to each audience, and instructive, as defined in Figure C below. Messaging that conveys only two or three of these elements, and not all four, will fall short of driving real change.

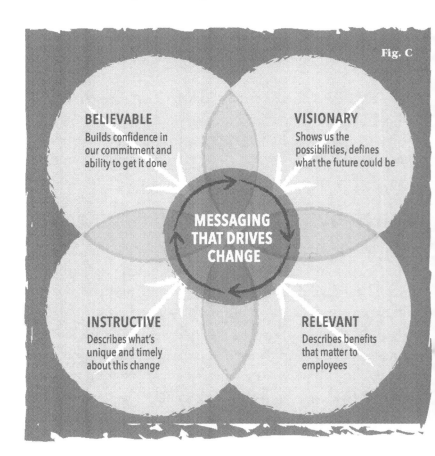

Fig. C

BELIEVABLE
Builds confidence in our commitment and ability to get it done

VISIONARY
Shows us the possibilities, defines what the future could be

MESSAGING THAT DRIVES CHANGE

INSTRUCTIVE
Describes what's unique and timely about this change

RELEVANT
Describes benefits that matter to employees

MAKE IT MEAN SOMETHING

Ask your employees to change and what do you think their first question will be? "Why?" It's logical that the reasons for the change should be included right off the bat, but many leaders fail to do this and instead lay out the vision, figuring they can get to their explanations later.

This not only rankles the modern employee—who requires a sense of meaning and ownership in his or her work—but also misses a big opportunity. If you explain why you're making a change, people will be much more likely to accept it than if you just spring the change on them with no reason to accompany it. The magic of combining change management strategies with communications is that if you have done the work of our prior steps, you are now well-positioned to explain why the change matters to your team.

He who has a why to live can bear almost any how.
Friedrich Nietschze

Take the example of one employee who went to pick up a document she'd printed at her regular, nearby printer only to find this: a sign taped to the printer with a tombstone reading "RIP" and a map to the printer she should now use, located down the hall. Huh?

There actually was a significant "why" for the choice to change printers that, if conveyed properly, would have demonstrated the value of the change. In fact, the printer changes—a smaller number of better, faster, user-friendly printers with all kinds of new capabilities—were part of a comprehensive overhaul of the company's technology. But the project team didn't link the incremental change to the larger story that smart technology, including upgraded desktops and other improvements, would help employees do their job more efficiently and improve productivity. A big mistake as far as making change meaningful.

We advise leaders to establish the reasons for the change at every opportunity, even after they tire of saying it. Remember the rule of seven—the time-tested marketing adage that says your audience needs to see your message seven times before adopting it—and then multiply it exponentially. Remind people of the context and benefits each time you ask for support, announce a new process step, or roll out a technology change. Keep in mind, as we established earlier, that employees weigh the effort involved in changing against the pain of the status quo.

TELL THE TRUTH

Employees are smart. They see through sugarcoating and know when you're avoiding important details. If a message isn't honest and straightforward, they'll parse the words and draw their own conclusions, which has enormous potential to derail a project.

Say what you can say and acknowledge what you can't. You've already removed the guesswork for dealing with each audience and therefore have insights into their concerns and questions. So deliver messaging that meets their needs and openly acknowledge when you can't. Sometimes you can't be entirely open because of legal requirements, federal trade regulations, or other legitimate reasons, and in that case, it's important to put that out there too, to be as transparent as possible.

Many leaders see honesty as a risk. They might be concerned about saying something too early that later must be corrected, or they might not want to acknowledge the truth even if everyone else already knows it. Every organization has a different level of risk tolerance. We've worked with clients with lengthy and onerous approval processes for even the most benign messages. Memos are reviewed by so many people that by the time they are ready to send, all specificity has been removed and the message is meaningless. Other organizations empower leaders to approve their own messages and press "send" without further review. No matter where your organization falls on that spectrum, the most important thing is to keep communicating honestly and share what you can as frequently as you can.

We worked with one CEO who did this beautifully. He wanted to communicate with his employees and build a trusting relationship with them. So, he started a weekly "Memo from Me." The tone was casual and open. He addressed questions from staff that normally a CEO might not think were worthy of answering. For example, in one of his early memos, he wrote about the company board meetings—something only the most senior leaders were able to attend. He explained in a clear, practical way how board meetings worked so that employees who had never attended one (read: most employees), could better understand the decision-making processes, activities, and priorities of a corporate board.

TEST BEFORE YOU SPEAK

"The CEO called me in his office and gave me a real 'dressing down.'"

"I've heard of casual Fridays but this is ridiculous!"

"I guess the emperor really does have no clothes."

These are just a few of the responses that resulted when a CEO forgot to test his messaging. This CEO had decided he was fed up with the way his employees dressed. He wanted to let them know that the company was instituting a new dress code, one that was, um, more buttoned-up.

The communications director had a great idea! You know those cardboard dolls of a person that you can dress in different outfits—you can get some these days that stick to the fridge? Let's make a doll in the likeness of the CEO and give out paper clothes—some work-appropriate and some not work-appropriate! The communications team (all of whom worked for the director) assembled to brainstorm, and they loved the idea. It was creative and cute and just what they needed to transmit the message about what was dignified office attire and what was not.

WHILE NEARLY ALL THOSE WE QUERIED IN OUR STUDY–APPROXIMATELY **98%**–FELT TESTING MESSAGING ON A SMALL SUBSET OF STAKEHOLDERS WAS IMPORTANT TO ESSENTIAL, ALMOST **1/2** FELT THEIR COMPANY DIDN'T DO IT WELL ENOUGH.

And then they gave their employees a cardboard paper doll of the CEO in his boxer shorts...ready to be dressed in paper clothes.

Need we go on?

We all know from experience that messages can miss the mark, cause confusion and result in all sorts of unintended consequences. You must test your messages with your intended audience before they ever see the light of day. Too time consuming? It doesn't have to be. You've identified your audiences in the last chapter. Often it takes only a quick meeting or two with representatives from each stakeholder group to learn valuable information that can turn a confusing or incomplete message into an effective communication.

GET EVERYONE SAYING THE SAME THING

An exciting new change gets everyone talking. At a minimum everyone involved on your project team, as well as your advisors, champions, and implementers, are all potential spokespeople for your initiative, and, in fact, should be encouraged to play that role. The key is getting them all to reinforce the same messages in their own words. You can't take for granted that because people are attending the team meetings or getting periodic briefings they are equipped to confidently speak about the project. If you don't provide them with the messages and materials and encourage them to share them, you miss an important opportunity.

Every initiative should have a defined message platform that clearly establishes the vision, objectives, key changes, benefits, timeline, and other critical elements to your particular project. This core set of messages provides the starting point for any subsequent communication about the program. To equip your team members and other spokespeople to carry the message, it is most effective to create a set of talking points and answers to anticipated questions. And as we pointed out earlier, remember to test these messages and answers with members of the target audience before providing them to the spokespeople.

IT PAYS TO TEST

We cannot overemphasize the importance of testing the messaging before going out to a wide audience. Testing is a simple step that costs little in the way of time or resources but can have a huge impact. Here are two examples.

Example 1

The first involved a large company we worked with to introduce a new skills credentialing program that allowed staff to apply for internal credentials at three levels in select disciplines. Just prior to launch, after we had developed the messaging but before we sent anything out, we tested the messaging with staff at all levels within the organization and with some of the company's clients. The feedback was invaluable and resulted in several subtle but important changes in the wording and tone of the communication materials. Below are some of the verbatim comments that came from staff members as they read proposed communications about the new program.

"Highlight the employee benefits first. Don't make me read through two paragraphs on why this is good for the company before I find out what might be appealing to me."

"Seems like the message is 'selling' the program, tone down the enthusiastic language and focus on the true benefits."

"The term 'talent development' sounds like something HR might say, but it doesn't mean anything to me."

"Information on the requirements and employee rewards comes too late in the presentation. Move it up closer to the front."

With this and other similar input the program was able to tailor its communication to be more effective with employees. **The investment of time resulted in a highly effective launch,** with nearly 2,000 employees visiting the program's intranet site in the first week to learn more.

Example 2

In another example, we supported an HR organization in the launch of a new online compensation statement. The statement gave employees a full view of the value of their compensation package, including base salary, insurance, training programs, and awards. The company's benefits package was top of the line but they were experiencing higher than expected attrition rates. So it was the leadership's hope that seeing the full value of benefits packages would engender greater employee loyalty and increase retention.

We expected a smooth launch and quick adoption. Not only did the statement provide valuable information, but it was also a great way to show employees the list of all available benefits— encouraging them to take advantage of additional perks that they hadn't been using. For example, many employees didn't avail themselves of tuition assistance or community service grants, or didn't know the firm offered adoption benefits and concierge service.

It seemed straightforward. But, just to be sure, we put the rosy messaging about this valuable new tool in front of a small test group of staffers. And a funny thing happened when we sat back and waited for the anticipated applause. The cynicism sounded like this:

"We know what this is about. You are just trying to convince us that it's okay to pay below market salaries because of all this other stuff."

"I can see my manager using this as a counter-offer when I threaten to quit, instead of increasing my salary."

"Thanks! This will be helpful for me to bring to my next job interview in order to compare offers."

The feedback also surfaced questions the project team had not anticipated. Employees wanted to know if they could be compensated for benefits they were not using. One employee asked, "Since I get dental benefits on my spouse's plan, can I be paid the equivalent in salary instead?"

The testing, which was conducted quickly through several short sessions over two weeks, brought to light some of the core issues impacting attrition, surfaced a tone of distrust and skepticism that was eye-opening, and identified unexpected staff questions about the policies reflected in the new compensation statement. If we hadn't gathered this feedback, our planned Pollyanna approach to the launch could have done more harm than good. Instead, we were able to make messaging changes that hit these issues head-on. The results: greater clarity about the purpose of the statement and greater sensitivity to the issues facing staff.

Want your messaging to be magic? Remember, no matter what you need to say, building language that is powerful, truthful, means something to your audience—and is vetted by a small representative group of your stakeholders—is the key to messaging success.

CHAPTER TEN

PREPARE THE STAKEHOLDERS

NOW YOU SEE IT (NOW YOU DON'T)

So, how's your change going so far? By this point, you should have built the big picture (hammering out with your project team a shared vision); removed the guesswork (identifying, categorizing, and analyzing your stakeholders); and gotten the message right (by creating and testing powerful, truthful, and well-targeted messaging). Whew.

So, now it's time to prepare the stakeholders—to arm them with the tools and materials they need to make the change. Hopefully by now you feel confident and ready.

But what if you hadn't done any of that previous work? Unfortunately, in typical change and communications efforts, that's exactly what happens. The approach looks something like this: a project team sits in a conference room a couple weeks before launch and someone starts writing on the white board, explaining, "Let's brainstorm on how to let people know about this."

Up to that point little advance work has been done and minimal thought given to the "people" part of the change. Sound familiar?

It's true that this step—prepare the stakeholders—is where the majority of work is to be done. We have to move our stakeholders through the three readiness stages—provide input, understand the changes, be prepared—via input sessions, focus groups, and a communications campaign. Granted, this is the visible, exciting work. But, the magic of our approach is that the work you do in those background steps, the work most of your people will never see, is critical to establishing the foundation for true accomplishment. As with any good magic trick, the effort is invisible to the audience. It only looks easy.

Beth learned this lesson during a volunteer mission to construct a training classroom at a drug and alcohol recovery center in Argentina. When she and the rest of the team arrived, the massive second floor space they were charged with refurbishing was an open, stifling hot, and nondescript white expanse. The light grey cement floor was covered with dust, the walls were lined with shoddily installed white drywall, and the arched ceiling was a simple tin roof. For three days the team worked to transform the room. It was

physically exhausting work as they carried heavy materials and equipment across the farm and upstairs to the workspace. They ripped off tape and dried spackle from the botched seams of the existing drywall and re-taped, sanded, and spackled the walls of the massive space again, and then sanded once more.

Despite an outside temperature topping 100 degrees and no air conditioning, the team climbed ladders to reach the ceiling area, feeling the temperature increase noticeably with each rung as they hung insulation and wires for a dropped ceiling frame. Three days into the labor, the room looked no different. The floor was still dust-encrusted cement. The walls where still white drywall. And the ceiling was still bare. Leaders and students from the facility would poke their head in from time to time and check out the progress. Although most nodded their approval, their eyes seemed to say, "What have they been doing for three days?"

On day four, the team climbed the ladders again to work on the dropped ceiling. To their surprise, the temperature was much more bearable. The insulation was doing its job. They attached brackets to the wires and, all of a sudden, there was a reliable frame in place from corner to corner to hold the ceiling tiles. Soon they had a checkerboard ceiling that was light and cool and transformed the space into something new. Change is like that. It is slow, sometimes exhausting, and requires stamina and perseverance. It takes time and sometimes it doesn't seem to be progressing until you take a step back and take it all in.

If the team had not labored those first three days—work that had little visible result—the final transformation would not have been possible. No one will ever see the tape, the insulation, or dropped wires again, but the benefits of the team's work will have lasting impact on all who use the space for decades to come.

As you advocate for an integrated change management and communications approach within your organization, you might find that you need to educate your leadership on the need for patience and sustained commitment during times when there is no visible progress. What they need to know is that this is the only way enduring change can be achieved.

If you've followed our recommended approach, you have also done the less visible hard work up front to build the big picture, remove the guesswork, and get the message right. You are now ready to create a solid, well-informed plan and execute it. A fully integrated communications and change management plan will guide the project team's actions in helping stakeholders embrace why the change is taking place, how it impacts them, and which actions are required. The plan should include all of the necessary tactics to effectively move stakeholders from awareness to understanding to action. It should also include the methods and timing for reaching each stakeholder.

COMMUNICATIONS AND CHANGE MANAGEMENT TOOLS FOR EVERY PLAN

Through our many years of aiding clients in managing change through the method and the magic approach, we've honed some communications and change management tactics to help you get your message across simply and clearly—and to deal with the resistance you might meet when folks don't want to hear it. The good news is, while we think they're magic, there's no sleight of hand involved. Just good, tried-and-true methods to get the work done.

COMMUNICATIONS TOOLS

- **Quick guides:** One- to two-page documents that can be easily accessed and used to summarize what folks need to do differently. You want to emphasize the "why" and then simply outline the steps—how to log on to the new system, how to review a new report, or what to do with the information once retrieved. We have often highlighted success stories and positive thoughts about the change on the margins of the guide.

- **FAQs:** These are a list of the questions you anticipate stakeholders will ask. We develop these by sitting in a room with the project team and coming up with what we think people will need to know. We then go out to talk with a few employees and give them a little information about the change and ask them, "What questions does this raise for you?" This is a great way to ensure that you have thought of everything (almost) that is going to be asked and can prepare all stakeholders in advance with the answer. When you are doing FAQs, include the real questions—don't gloss over the truth.

- **Training materials:** Make sure you engage your organization's learning and development team to assist with training. They will help you decide the best medium for the type of learning that needs to take place. Some changes require classroom training, for others online modules will do, and for others the change might be so intuitive that your quick guide will suffice.

- **Briefing decks with notes:** Briefing decks with notes are the best way to make sure that all presenters on the topic of your change are telling the story consistently from group to group. Prepare a key message deck that outlines what is changing and why, what happens if we don't change, what the benefits of the change are, and any actions they need to take. Add talking points or a presenter script so that the deck can stand alone and can be used consistently, regardless of who is presenting.

- **Articles, blogs, and memos:** These are other ways to get the message out and the content and flavor will depend on the audience and the vehicle itself. From an article, blog, or e-mail, you can always point people to the other materials mentioned above.

- **Follow-up office hours:** We have seen this work very successfully as a post-implementation tactic. Roll out the change and then have key implementers available to answer questions or show people how to do advanced operations with the new system.

RESOURCES FOR MANAGING RESISTANCE

You will encounter resistance—it's a natural human response to change. The first step is to identify it. Peter Block, in his book *Flawless Consulting*, provides great tips and techniques for dealing with it once you do (Block, 2000). We highly recommend you read Block's book. Here are some tips on how we deal with resistance, inspired by his advice.

FORM OF RESISTANCE	SUGGESTED RESPONSE
Too much information	"You are giving me more information than I need. Can you describe it in a few words?"
Too little information	"You are being very brief. Can you say more?"
Evasiveness	"We're getting off topic. Let's focus on the task at hand."
Over-eagerness	"You're being so agreeable, it's hard to tell what you really think."
Reticence	"You're keeping to yourself. I don't know how to read your reticence."
Relentlessness	"We're not ready to find the answers yet. I'm still trying to find out [insert the issue you are addressing]…"
Aggressiveness	"You are challenging many pieces of this change. Is something bothering you?"

ENGAGING STAKEHOLDERS

What you need to do to make the change happen—help your stakeholders provide input, understand the changes, and be prepared—is reliant on engaging stakeholders properly. This transition is not something you are doing to them; it is something you are doing with them. Chapter Five, Remove the Guesswork, established what makes your stakeholder groups tick and the reasons for enlisting them. This chapter will show you how to leverage them in a thoughtful and powerful way.

There is no one right way to engage with and prepare stakeholders, no one-size-fits-all approach. You must dive in with the knowledge and insights you've gained in the first three steps. It sounds intimidating but if you've been following all of our previous steps and advice, you will be fine.

For each stakeholder group we create a wide-ranging plan to engage them through the transition. As you create yours, remember the purposes behind each stage. You want to first get stakeholders to provide input through involvement and ideas, creating an early signal to the organization about the nature of the change. Second, you want to help stakeholders understand the changes by getting them to see the "why" behind the transition, removing barriers that might impede their support, and positioning them well to accept and even embrace the change. And lastly, you want your stakeholders to be prepared for the launch, instructing them about new requirements and expectations, and providing necessary information and support through training and easy-to-use tools such as guides.

As discussed below, the approach to moving each group through the readiness steps must be tailored for each stakeholder type. Each group will be brought in at different points in the project lifecycle and will need distinct messages and communications tactics. Let's take it from the top: advisors.

ADVISORS

 **Advisors are your leaders.** They understand the nature of the problem your transition will address. They are generally high-ranking within the organization and have a grasp of the long view—and often the benefit of a 360-degree view—of the organization. They will help shape your solution from vision to implementation.

We have found that this is not a group that you need to be overly creative in reaching. They are the leadership, or have been selected by it, and that gives them "skin in the game."

Your first advisor will likely be your executive sponsor. But one leader is rarely sufficient to shape a complex solution. Even if the executive sponsor has a compelling vision and wields significant power, you'll need a set of leaders with diverse viewpoints and who are empowered to make decisions on behalf of the organization.

TIPS FOR LEVERAGING YOUR ADVISORS

- Do your homework prior to meeting with this group. Once you're in front of them, be brief and be gone.

- Think like an executive. Be relevant—unless you want to be picked apart and questioned.

- Appoint from among your advisors a steering committee with diverse leadership. Make time for members to share their individual work with peers so the committee has an organization-wide perspective.

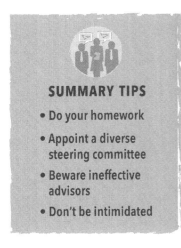

SUMMARY TIPS

- Do your homework
- Appoint a diverse steering committee
- Beware ineffective advisors
- Don't be intimidated

- Beware of ineffective advisors. Partway through the effort you may find one of your advisors is not contributing to your change efforts for any of a number of reasons. He may lack decision-making power, be highly political, or have a parochial view. Make a mid-course correction with the help of your executive sponsor.

- And lastly, don't be intimidated. As one of our CEO clients says,

"We put our shoes and socks on the same way in the C-suite."
Or as Mike Brady said in *The Brady Bunch*, "Picture them in
their underwear." But, remember, don't take this literally as the
ill-fated CEO paper doll experiment did!

CHAMPIONS

**Your champions play an integral role as
the voice of your transformation.** These are
the people who will communicate the changes
to the rest of the organization. Your advisors will
play this spokesperson role as well, but every
change needs people on the ground, closer to the employees, to
influence and sustain change. In any organization there are
influencers at all levels—people who are respected and listened
to by their peers, who are well liked and followed. Influencers
generally distinguish themselves early on by their contributions
to discussions in the first few steps—they are generally engaged
and outspoken.

Finding your influencers and convincing them to be champions
can be a challenge. Asking advisors to enlist the help of influencers can be effective. Your advisors also will naturally point
them out, saying something like, "Talk to Jamie in Accounting,
she's a rock star." Or, "Brad in Marketing always knows what's
going on with everyone, check in with him." Use these influ-
ential people as champions.

TIPS FOR EQUIPPING CHAMPIONS

- Sometimes a vocal naysayer can be your most effective champion. Not all naysayers can be converted, but be on the lookout for leaders who, with the right understanding of the transition, may switch sides and benefit the program greatly.

- You need to equip your champions with thorough background knowledge of the project and its progress, but you don't want them to be too scripted. You must help them appear prepared but not robotic. The messaging must be authentic and in their voice for it to be effective with their co-workers.

SUMMARY TIPS

- Convert a naysayer
- Equip champions thoroughly
- Test authentic message thoroughly beforehand

- Because you have tested the message prior to this point to uncover problems with your messaging, you shouldn't have any surprises. You should know where potential criticism might crop up and how to prepare your champions to manage it.

IMPLEMENTERS

Implementers are helpers and doers. Implementers are subject matter experts regarding the technical component of the change, and knowledgeable about your project team and other groups who will be responsible for making sure the new way of doing things sticks. For this reason, they require different support, depending on the nature of the transition. They must understand what is going on and unapologetically explain the changes to impacted employees.

Reaching this group is often not difficult because implementing the change is a key part of their job. For example, the job of the IT help desk is to troubleshoot questions and problems with systems. So if you are phasing in new software, their task remains the same, but they need to go through the readiness stages in order to respond to user questions appropriately. The same goes for a financial transition. You're going to look to employees in your finance group to do their same functions—just in the service of the change.

TIPS FOR TRAINING IMPLEMENTERS

• Let them know you need their knowledge and expertise to shape the rollout plan. Most people love to have their knowledge recognized and used. Implementers can be your most potent assets, if well utilized.

- Provide solid tools such as presentation decks with talking points and notes, training in new processes or systems, frequently asked questions documents, quick reference guides, and summary sheets or tip cards that highlight changes and required actions.

- Reach implementers during their standard department meetings or by memos and e-mail messages with pertinent information clearly outlined.

- Provide a forum for implementers to air their feelings and potential frustrations in dealing with impacted groups. One project team offered office hours and a series of open conference calls that implementers could join so they could get questions answered, vent about (sometimes wacky) user complaints and laugh about them, and settle back into their role as helpers.

SUMMARY TIPS
- Utilize implementers well
- Provide solid tools
- Deliver concise information
- Provide a forum
- Learn their beliefs
- Prepare them well

- Learn what this group believes is critical to a successful launch and what their experiences are with the impacted group.

- Educate your implementers about what impacted groups need to know and how they can help support them. This group doesn't just need to be prepared—they need to be super-prepared.

IMPACTED GROUPS

 **As the name suggests, impacted groups are all the people who must do something differently as a result of the change.** Different might mean a new process, a new system, a new technology, a new office location, or even a new traffic pattern—or it might be that they need to stop doing something. They may even be losing their jobs. The change will most directly and dramatically impact these folks, so it is critical that they are involved in every stage. In many ways, how they adapt to and adopt the change is the litmus test of your initiative's success.

It's important to learn what this group thinks of the change solution—the merits and downsides, barriers that might get in their way, what might help carry the change. You will get better solutions if you tap into this group early on.

If you are implementing a change that impacts many thousands of people, you'll want to work with a sample of this group. We are not suggesting surveying all the people in impacted groups. Select a diverse group who represent appropriate demographics (e.g., tenure, gender, geography, management level, and role), and use them as a regular sounding board to determine how to discuss the solution, message, and tactics with other employees.

TIPS FOR PREPARING IMPACTED GROUPS

• Anticipate the emotional response to change and consider rituals that will help employees process their feelings about letting go of the old and embracing the new. For example, when one company moved from a downtown location to the suburbs, they handed out keys to the new office on keychains made from pieces of their old office.

• Gauging the reaction of impacted groups to the change is critical. You can do this by querying a representative sample in focus groups and user acceptance tests, and through surveys or at social events.

• Impacted groups need to be clear on what is changing, why it is changing, and what the problem is with NOT changing. This is where the four characteristics of balanced messaging are so important. For a reminder, take another look at the graphic on page 82.

SUMMARY TIPS
• Anticipate emotional responses to change
• Gauge reaction
• Emphasize balanced messaging
• Provide clear training & instructions
• Be visible with initiatives
• Recruit volunteers
• Offer training pre- and post-change

- Training, webinars, reference guides, tip sheets, FAQs, and standard operating procedures (SOP) are a great way to help them prepare. Be clear and instructive in the message. Tell people exactly how they need to behave, what they need to do, and who to call if they need help.

- Show up in the workplace to gather feedback. For example, hold impromptu focus groups during breaks in the company training facility, buy impacted groups lunch, or offer a coffee shop gift card for participating in data collection efforts.

- Ask for volunteers to be part of a survey group that periodically receives electronic questionnaires.

- Consider offering training for impacted groups both before the change occurs and after implementation when they can ask more detailed questions.

CHAPTER ELEVEN

EVALUATE THE RESULTS (AND SAVOR SUCCESS)

YOU'VE CHANGED!

When you started reading, we asked you to imagine that you were tapped to lead an important change initiative for your organization and then we promised to help you through it. We hope you've gotten the information, tools, and ideas you need to face it with confidence and competence.

Now it's time for the final step of the method and the magic: evaluate the results. Don't let evaluation make you nervous. We understand; we told you from the beginning how high the stakes are for organizational change. How leaders can manage it poorly, endangering the longevity of companies and careers. But if you followed the steps, evaluation shouldn't put fear into your heart, because we—and you—have had our eyes on the prize the whole time.

Each step of the way, we've asked ourselves what success looked like from the perspectives of both the business and the stakeholder. From the moment we built a

> **"Changes of any sort—even though they may be justified in economic or technological terms—finally succeed or fail on the basis of whether or not the people affected do things differently."**
>
> Bridges, 2003

shared vision to the moment when our well-prepared team realized it, we constantly checked in, and checked ourselves. We don't need to look hard for our results because we can trust that by using an integrated change management and communications method we've covered all the bases.

To create the scoreboard for success, marry the expected business benefits with the desired behaviors of each group and the definition of "prepared" for each group. Together these measures—some qualitative and some quantitative—define success.

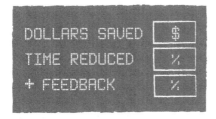

Create the scorecard and gain buy-in. Come back to the scorecard regularly throughout the project and compare what you are hearing from stakeholders with your desired state. Adjust your strategy along the way if your feedback and observed actions are not in line with your scorecard.

No surprises! You don't just measure at the end; you measure the whole way through. That is the beauty of integrated communications and change management—the constant feedback mechanism. We've continually measured success by engaging with our stakeholders—and having our finger on the pulse of our change. Change takes hold in stages, but because we are gauging our success on previously defined benchmarks, we can trust that we're heading in the right direction.

We recommend evaluating your results even after the transition has taken place, at three-, six-, nine- and twelve-month intervals. We find the Kirkpatrick Model helpful in evaluation and think you might, too. According to an article in *Chief Learning Officer*, "Don Kirkpatrick wrote the book on evaluation in learning and development, literally." Developed in the 1950s, the model outlines four levels of evaluation and still sets the standard. The four levels are:

1) **Reaction**: what impacted groups think about the training and preparation for change

2) **Learning**: their increase in knowledge or capability

3) **Behavior**: the extent of behavior capability and implementation

4) **Results**: the effect on the business resulting from the change in impacted groups' performance (Margolis, 2009).

Using the Kirkpatrick Model you can gauge how each of your stakeholders meet the four benchmarks.

These are mainly qualitative results but we don't need to doubt our results just because they're not entirely quantitative. They don't need to be. Yes, you are welcome to analyze data about the success of your cost-cutting initiative or whether users adopted a new payroll system, and you certainly should. But this analysis won't tell you the whole story. The rest of the story will be told on the way to the cafeteria when a user of your new software system stops you in the hall and says, "I hated the idea of switching over, and I was comfortable with the old system, but now I can't imagine doing my work without the new one. It's so much better!"

The true measure of success for your change will come down to something basic. You have groups of people who've been asked to think, feel, and do things differently. If you've used our method, with some of our magic sprinkled in, you should see a transformed process or organization, and people who are on board and moving forward.

WORKS CITED

Block, Peter. *The Empowered Manager: Positive Political Skills at Work*. San Francisco: Jossey Bass, 1987.

Block, Peter. *Flawless Consulting: A Guide to Getting Your Expertise Used*. San Francisco: Jossey-Bass/Pfeiffer, 2000. Internet resource.

Bridges, William. *Managing Transitions, Making the Most of Change*. 3rd Edition. Boston: De Capo Press, 2009.

Cohen, Dan S. *The Heart of Change Field Guide*. Boston: Harvard Business Press, 2005.

IBM. *Survey of 1,500 Change Management Executives*. October, 2008.

Kanter, Rosabeth M. "Seven Truths about Change to Live By." *Harvard Business Review*, 2010. Accessed February, 2015: https://hbr.org/2010/08/seven-truths-about-change-to-l/

Kanter, Rosabeth M. *The Change Masters: Innovation for Productivity in the American Corporation*. New York: Simon & Schuster, 1983.

Kenison, Katrina. *The Gift of an Ordinary Day*. New York: Grand Central Publishing, 2009.

Kotter, John. *A Sense of Urgency*. Boston: Harvard Business Press, 2008.

Kouzes, James and Posner, Barry. "To Lead, Create a Shared Vision." *Harvard Business Review*, 2009. Accessed September, 2014: http://hbr.org/2009/01/to-lead-create-a-shared-vision/ar/1

Logica Management Consulting: Survey of 380 Senior Executives in Western Europe, October, 2008.

Lokker, Brian. "U.S. Coffee Rationing in World War II." *Coffee Crossroads*, January, 2013. Accessed September, 2014: http://www.coffeecrossroads.com/coffee-history/u-s-coffee-rationing-in-world-war-ii

Margolis, Daniel. "The Father of the Four Levels." *Chief Learning Officer*: November, 2009. Accessed September 4, 2014.

McKinsey & Company in conjunction with the University of Oxford: Study on large scale IT Projects, October, 2012.

Senge, Peter M. *The Fifth Discipline: The Art and Practice of the Learning Organization*. New York: Doubleday/Currency, 1990.

Beth McDonald, President, The Wheelhouse Group and Laurie Axelrod, President, LEA Consulting Group

With more than 40 years of consulting experience between them, Laurie Axelrod and Beth McDonald advise top executives in federal agencies and large commercial enterprises on how to effectively communicate change in order to drive new behaviors and improve business performance. They each lead successful consulting businesses serving public and private sector clients: LEA Consulting Group (Laurie) and The Wheelhouse Group (Beth). Together, they created the integrated change management and communications method they and their teams put into practice every day. They share this effective method—and a little magic—with you in *The Method and The Magic: Every Leader's Guide to Making Transformational Change Happen.*

46271520R00073

Made in the USA
Charleston, SC
14 September 2015